This Handwriting Notebook Belongs To:

A

A is For

Ex: abeja

B

B is For

Ex: botas

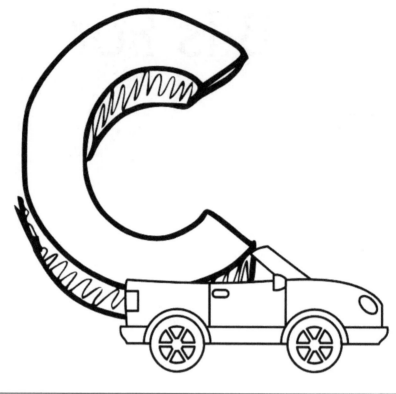

C is For

Ex: carro

Ch is For

Ex: chile

D is For

Ex: dinosaurio

E is For

Ex: elephante

F is For

Ex: flor

G is For

Ex: gato

H is For

Ex: helado

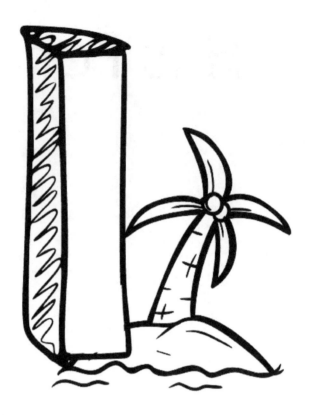

I

I is For

Ex: isla

J

J is For

Ex: jirafa

K is For

Ex: koala

L is For

Ex: limón

Ll

LL is For

Ex: llave

M is For

Ex: manzana

N is For

Ex: nido

O is For

Ex: oso

P

P is For

Ex: pastel

Q is For

Ex: queso

R is For

Ex: rato

s

S is For

Ex: silla

T is For

Ex: tortuga

U is For

Ex: unicornio

V is For

Ex: vaca

W is For

Ex: wafle

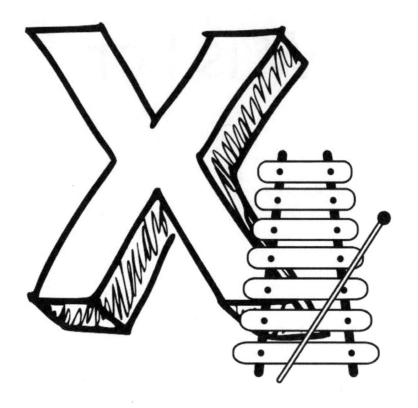

X is For

Ex: xilófono

Y

Y is For

Ex: yoyo

z

Z is For

Ex: zapatos

www.ingramcontent.com/pod-product-compliance
Lightning Source LLC
LaVergne TN
LVHW081229230125
801973LV00025B/516